D1607215

ANCIENT ROMAN SPORTS AND PASTIMES

Nicola Barber

PowerKiDS
press.

New York

Published in 2010 by The Rosen Publishing Group Inc.
29 East 21st Street, New York, NY 10010

Copyright © 2010 Wayland/The Rosen
Publishing Group, Inc.

First Edition

Series Editor: Julia Adams
Editor: Penny Worms
Series Consultant: Sally Pointer, archaeologist
Designer: Jane Hawkins
Picture Researcher: Kathy Lockley

Library of Congress Cataloging-in-Publication Data

Barber, Nicola.
  Ancient Roman sports and pastimes / Nicola Barber.
    p. cm. -- (Ancient communities: Roman life)
  Includes index.
  ISBN 978-1-61532-306-7 (library binding)
  ISBN 978-1-61532-315-9 (paperback)
  ISBN 978-1-61532-316-6 (6-pack)
  1. Games--Rome--Juvenile literature. 2. Sports--Rome--Juvenile literature.
  3. Rome--Social life and customs--Juvenile literature. I. Title.
  GV31.B37 2010
  796.0937--dc22

                          2009023744

Photographs:
akg-images: 14; Derek Croucher/Alamy: 19;
Art Archive/Corbis: Title page, 9, 13, 18;
Bridgeman Art Library/Getty Images: COVER
(main), 11, 15; Gianni Dagli Orti/The Art
Archive: 24; C.M.; Dixon/Heritage-Images: 22;
Mary Evans Picture Library/Alamy: 16, 17; Chris
Hellier/Corbis: 20; ImageState/Alamy: 6; Mimmo
Jodice/Corbis: 7, 18, 29; London Art Archive/
Alamy: COVER (inset), 5, 10, 21, 28; Musee
National, Beirut, Lebanon/Giraudon/Bridgeman
Art Library, London: 23; Pergamon Museum, Berlin,
Germany/Bridgeman Art Library, London: 4, 27; Premier/Alamy: 25;
The Print Collector/Alamy: 8, 26; Ron Sachs/CNP/Corbis: 12

Manufactured in China

CPSIA Compliance Information: Batch #WAW0102PK: For Further Information

contact Rosen Publishing, New York, New York at 1-800-237-9932

Contents

Words in **bold** can be found in the glossary.

The Roman Empire

Around 2,000 years ago, the Romans built a huge empire that stretched from Britain in the north to Egypt in the south. The Romans introduced their ways of life to people all across their empire.

Beginnings

The Romans were originally a tribe of **Latin**-speaking people who lived in the west of central Italy. According to legend, the city of Rome was founded in 753 BCE. At first, Rome was ruled by kings, but in 509 BCE, the Romans set up a **republic**. This was a new kind of government in which male Roman **citizens** voted to elect their leaders. In 27 BC, Octavian took control and became Rome's first emperor. The Romans built roads across their vast empire to allow their armies to march quickly from one place to another. They also built grand public buildings, such as **amphitheaters**. As a result, people who lived many thousands of miles away from Rome began to adopt Roman ways of life.

The Colosseum in Rome was one of the largest amphitheaters built by the Romans. It could hold up to 50,000 spectators.

Work and leisure

A typical working day began at dawn, when Romans went out to start their daily business. For most people, the main meal of the day was in the evening. There were no "weekends" when people did not work, but there were many public holidays in the Roman year. These were often festival days, or days of public celebration when people flocked to the **chariot** races and amphitheaters.

⇧ This wall painting shows a scene in a tavern. Roman taverns were popular places for drinking, eating, and gambling.

Written at the time

The Roman poet, Juvenal, wrote about the two things that ordinary Romans were most interested in:

"Now two things only do they [the Roman people] ardently desire: bread and chariot races in the Circus."

Chariot racing

All over the Roman Empire, people loved to spend their leisure time at the races. Chariot racing was hugely popular with people of all **social classes**, from slaves to emperors.

The race

Chariot races were held on an oval racetrack, called a *circus*. Down the middle of the racetrack was a barrier, called the *spina*, with tall posts at each end. The **charioteers** usually raced seven times around the *spina*, turning as fast as they dared around the posts. There were markers on the *spina*, often in the shapes of dolphins or eggs. After each lap, one of these markers was turned upside down or removed to show the charioteers how many laps were left in the race.

These chariots are being pulled by four horses, the usual number for chariot races. Some races were for two- or three-horse teams, and some for six or even more!

This is a four-horse chariot team.

A Roman object

This mosaic celebrates a victorious team from the Reds. The charioteer (in the middle) has been presented with a palm branch to show that he is the winner. The team and the driver also received money for their win. The charioteer's short-sleeved tunic and his leather helmet were worn to give some protection to his head in the event of a crash.

Following a team

Chariot racing was fast and furious. There were often accidents as chariots overturned or crashed into each other. In Rome, all of the charioteers belonged to one of four teams—the Whites, Reds, Greens, or Blues. People had a favorite team, just like fans of football teams today. There was particular **rivalry** between the Greens, which was mainly backed by the ordinary people, and the Blues, the team of choice for Roman leaders.

Gladiator fights

On public holidays and other special occasions, Roman rulers put on lavish shows to entertain the people. These shows included battles, often to the death, between trained fighters called **gladiators**.

Gladiators

Almost every large town or city across the Roman Empire had its own large, open-air amphitheater. This is where the gladiator fights took place. Most gladiators were slaves, convicted criminals, or prisoners of war. They were trained to fight at special gladiator schools.

There were various types of gladiators, each using different armor and weapons. Some carried short, stabbing swords, others fought with longer swords. One type of gladiator, called a *retarius*, was armed with only a net and a trident (a three-pronged spear).

This bronze gladiator's helmet is designed to protect the wearer from his opponent.

Written at the time

These words were written (in Latin) on the tombstone of a gladiator named Flamma by a fellow gladiator, Delicatus:

"Flamma ... lived 30 years, fought 34 times, won 21 times, fought to a draw 9 times, defeated 4 times, a Syrian by nationality. Delicatus made this for his deserving comrade-in-arms."

The fight

The Roman public loved the gory spectacle of a gladiator fight. People in the audience shouted and screamed to encourage the gladiators. A fight usually lasted until one gladiator became badly wounded or surrendered. At this point, if the crowd thought the defeated gladiator had fought bravely, it would shout, "Let him go!" However, the final decision was up to the **sponsor** of the games, often the emperor himself. He signaled with his thumb whether or not the defeated gladiator should be killed.

⊘ A gladiator pins his opponent to the ground and prepares to strike a final blow with his short, stabbing sword.

BELLEREFONS

PIDO

AURIVS

MELIA

P

Wild animal shows

The lavish shows put on in Roman amphitheaters also featured fights with wild beasts. The animals were made to fight each other, or they were hunted and killed by trained fighters.

Capturing the animals

Animals were brought to Rome from all over the Empire and beyond for these shows. They included elephants, panthers, lions, tigers, bears, hippopotamuses, and ostriches. In some places, so many animals were captured and taken for the Roman games that very few remained in the wild.

The Colosseum in Rome was designed specially for wild animal shows. Beneath the floor of the **arena** lay a network of cages and tunnels where the wild beasts were kept before the show.

This is a view of the tunnels and cage entrances beneath the Colosseum in Rome.

Bloody shows

Fights with wild animals were often the morning's entertainment before a gladiator show in the afternoon. Huge numbers of animals died in the wild animal shows. When the Colosseum was officially opened in 80 CE, there were 100 days of games, during which around 9,000 animals died. Sometimes the animals were hunted in a pretend forest, created by shrubs and trees that were placed around the arena. At other times, convicted criminals were executed by being forced into the arena, where they were torn to pieces by the animals.

⬆ This wall painting shows a fighter facing an extremely fierce-looking lion at a Roman wild beast show.

Written at the time

The Roman historian, Cassius Dio, gave this account of a wild animal show held in honor of Emperor Septimius Severus in 204 CE:

"At this time there occurred...all sorts of spectacles in honor of Severus' return, the completion of his first ten years of power, and his victories...there came rushing forth bears, lionesses, panthers, lions, ostriches, wild asses, bisons...so that seven hundred beasts in all, both wild and domesticated, at one and the same time were seen running about and were slaughtered."

Sea battles

Some Roman emperors spent huge amounts on specially staged sea fights. These shows often told the stories of real sea fights that had happened earlier in history.

Caesar's show

The first sea battles that we know about was held by Julius Caesar in 46 BCE. It was held to celebrate various victories over his rivals. He ordered a lake to be dug just outside Rome. Then small ships, called **galleys**, were launched onto the lake. The galleys were manned by thousands of prisoners of war, who were forced to fight each other.

This stone sculpture shows a Roman galley, or warship. Small versions of these ships were used for staged sea fights.

Written at the time

In *The Lives of the Caesars*, the Roman historian, Suetonius, describes Caesar's staged sea battle in 46 BCE:

"For the naval battle, a pool was dug…and there was a contest of ships of two, three, and four banks of oars, belonging to the Tyrian [from Tyre in the eastern Mediterranean] and Egyptian fleets, manned by a large force of fighting men. Such a throng flocked to all these shows from every quarter, that many strangers had to lodge in tents pitched in streets or along the roads, and the press was often such that many were crushed to death, including two senators."

This staged sea fight is being held in a flooded amphitheater. We do not know for certain whether the Colosseum was flooded for such spectacles.

Lavish spectacles

Emperor Augustus staged a sea battle in 2 BCE that told the story of an actual battle between the Athenians and the Persians that took place in 480 BCE. Augustus also had a lake specially dug for this battle. Another emperor, Claudius, staged one of the biggest sea battles that we know about. There were more than 100 ships, and around 19,000 men took part, most of them convicted criminals. It is also possible that the Colosseum was partly flooded for mock battles.

Track and field and exercise

The Romans were keen on track and field events and games to keep the body fit. "A healthy body and a healthy mind" was a well-known Roman saying.

The Games

The Romans got their interest in track and field events from the Greeks. The ancient Olympic games started in Greece in 776 BCE. They were held every four years as part of a religious festival. Athletes came from all over Greece to compete for prizes. The Olympic Games continued after Greece became part of the Roman Empire, until they were **banned** in 393 CE. The Romans established their own games, the Capitoline Games, in 86 CE. Like the Olympic Games, they were held every four years. Prizes were given for running races, boxing, wrestling, and throwing the javelin. There were also prizes for poetry and music.

These athletes are taking part in a discus-throwing competition. Discus throwing was one of the events included in the Capitoline Games.

Exercising

Wrestling and boxing were favorite pastimes. Wrestlers covered themselves in a mixture of oil and wax called *ceroma*, then dusted themselves with soft sand to make it more difficult for their opponents to get a good grip. Ball games were also popular, particularly throwing and catching games. The Romans built gymnasiums for people to take exercise. Often, these gymnasiums were attached to public baths, so that people could bathe after exercising.

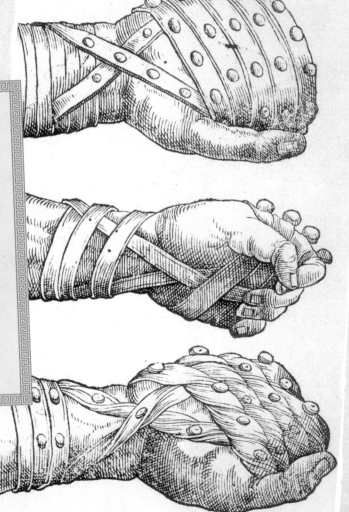

A Roman object

Boxing was a popular sport in Roman times. In early times, boxers wrapped pieces of leather (thongs) around their hands and wrists for protection during the fight. As time went on, these thongs were made from harder leather, and then spikes and studs were added, as shown here. A Roman boxing match was often a fight to the death. Boxing was eventually banned in the Roman Empire.

These are leather thongs wrapped around a boxer's hands. The thongs are covered in studs designed to injure an opponent.

The theater

People of all social classes enjoyed a visit to the theater in Roman times. But the theater was never as popular as a day at the races or gladiator fights at the local amphitheater.

On the stage

The Romans copied and adapted Greek theater traditions, and many of the actors were from Greece. Roman audiences liked to be entertained and amused, so **comedies** were much more popular than **tragedies**. The actors wore masks and fooled around on stage to please their audiences. **Mime** was a favorite type of comedy, performed without masks.

In Roman mime the actors spoke, unlike modern-day mime shows, which are silent. The Romans also invented pantomime, but this was different compared to the pantomime we know today. In a Roman pantomime, a masked actor performed the actions, and singers and musicians told the story.

This wall painting shows two Roman actors who have just taken off their masks after a performance.

Terence
195 BC–159 BC

Terence is one of the best-known Roman playwrights. He was born a slave in North Africa and was taken to Rome by his master, a senator named Terentius Lucanus. The senator was so impressed by his slave's abilities that he educated him, and later freed him from slavery. Terence is remembered for comic plays, such as *The Girl from Andros*, *Phormio*, *The Brothers*, and *Her Husband's Mother*.

Roman theaters

There were theaters in many Roman towns and cities. These were usually open-air buildings, although **awnings** were sometimes put up to protect the audience from the sunshine or rain. A typical theater had a curved bank of seats on one side, looking toward a raised stage area backed by a wall. There were usually three doors in the wall for the actors to make their entrances and exits.

The Roman amphitheater in Orange, France, is one of the best preserved in the world.

Music

Music was very important in the Roman theater and at Roman festivals. It was also used in religious ceremonies and in the Roman army.

Musical instruments

The Romans played a variety of instruments, many borrowed or adapted from Greece or other regions of the Empire. Stringed instruments included the **lyre** and the *kithara*, both played by **plucking** the strings. A popular wind instrument was the *aulos*. This was a pipe with reeds in its mouthpiece that **vibrated** as the player blew. The pipes were usually played in pairs, with the player holding one pipe in each hand.

⬇ This Roman mosaic shows the Greek hero, Orpheus, playing his lyre. The lyre was a popular stringed instrument in Greek and Roman times.

A Roman object

The *hydraulis* was one of the earliest keyboard instruments. It had metal pipes set on top of a wind chest. Air was pumped out of the wind chest into the pipes to make a sound. The player pushed keys, or on some instruments, pulled sliders in and out, to let air into the pipes. The *hydraulis* became very popular in Roman times. It was played in theaters, at festivals, and in amphitheaters to accompany gladiator shows.

This mosaic shows two men playing music. The right-hand man is playing a curved horn called a cornu. The left-hand man is playing a type of early organ called a *hydraulis*.

The importance of music

Although music was a popular form of entertainment, most educated Romans thought that musicians were no higher than actors on the social scale. Rich Romans liked to employ musicians to perform at private parties, often with groups of dancers. Musicians played during performances at the theater, and also in the amphitheaters during gladiator shows. Music was an important part of the many Roman festivals, and pipes were usually played at religious ceremonies.

Food and entertainment

Most Romans normally ate little as they went about their business during the day. The evening meal, called the *cena*, was the Romans' main meal.

Rich and poor

Many ordinary Romans did not have kitchens, so they bought cooked food from shops called *thermopolia*. The diet for most Romans centered around bread, **cereals**, and vegetables. Well-to-do Romans ate a wider variety of foods and they loved to show off their wealth at dinner parties. Many rich Romans had trained cooks who produced elaborate dishes using exotic ingredients. Fish and meat were often served with spicy sauces—probably because it was very difficult to keep food fresh, and these sauces helped to disguise the taste!

This wall painting of a banquet shows the guests lying on sofas to make them comfortable. The food and wine are being served by slaves.

Written at the time

In his work *Satyricon*, the Roman writer, Petronius, described the elaborate dishes presented to guests at a dinner party:

"Dormice seasoned with honey and poppies... sausages brought in piping hot on a silver **gridiron**, and under that, Syrian plums and pomegranate grains... stuffed capons [roosters], a sow's paps, and as a centerpiece, a hare fitted with wings to represent Pegasus [a winged horse]..."

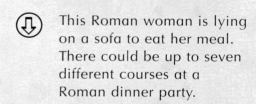

Dinner parties

At a Roman dinner party, the guests lay on couches arranged around a low table. Servants would bring the food. There could be as many as seven different courses, including appetizers, several courses of fish and meat, and fresh fruit and nuts for dessert. Diners had knives and spoons (there were no forks), but mostly they ate with their right hands, which they washed frequently in bowls brought by the servants. There was often entertainment, such as dancing, clowning, or poetry-reading between courses.

⬇ This Roman woman is lying on a sofa to eat her meal. There could be up to seven different courses at a Roman dinner party.

Public bathhouses

The Romans built large public bathhouses in towns and cities all over their empire. Few Roman houses had their own bathrooms, so a visit to the baths was an important part of many Romans' leisure time.

A social occasion

For the Romans, a visit to the bathhouses was also a chance see friends. Men and women bathed at separate times—men often visited the baths on their way home before the evening meal; women usually went in the morning. In some places, there were separate baths for men and women. People went to the baths after exercising in the gymnasium, to relax, to swim, and to clean themselves.

 This mosaic shows a man getting dressed during a visit to the baths. Slaves are on hand to help him.

Written at the time

In his work about Roman buildings, *De Architetura*, the **architect**, Vitruvius, described how the hot water needed for public baths was heated in massive containers by a fire:

"The cauldrons over the furnaces are to be three in number, one for hot water, another for tepid water, and a third for cold water: and they must be so arranged, that hot water which runs out of the heated vessel, may be replaced by an equal quantity from the tepid vessel, which in like manner is supplied from the cold vessel, and that the arched cavities in which they stand may be heated by one fire."

Hot, warm, and cold

A visit to the baths started in the changing rooms, where people left their clothes. Bathers were then rubbed down with oil, before spending some time exercising in the gymnasium.

⬆ The Great Bath in the city of Bath, U.K., was—and still is—fed by a natural hot spring.

After the gymnasium, people first visited a hot, steamy room called the *caldarium*. Here, the bather sweated even more in the heat, and the accumulated sweat and dirt was scraped off, usually by a slave, with a curved metal tool called a *strigil*. The bather then moved to a warm room, and then to a cold room, where there was often a cold pool to plunge into. The Romans believed that bathing in cold water was good for the health.

Children's pastimes

Many Roman children had little time to play. Children from poor families and slaves' children were put to work from an early age. In well-to-do families, most children divided their time between education and leisure.

Education

Some young children were taught at home, often by educated Greek slaves. Other children went to school where they learned to read and write. Most girls, however, learned little more than the basics before their education came to an end. It was considered more important for girls to learn how to run the household from their mothers. A few boys continued their studies into their teens, learning about Greek and Roman literature, and the skills needed for public speaking.

A young girl reads from a scroll. Roman girls learned to read and write and to keep household accounts.

A Roman object

Knucklebones was a popular game, played with bones from a sheep or pig. The different parts of the bone had different values, and the player threw the bone onto a table, then counted the value of the side on which it fell. This game was very popular with girls.

At play

Roman children played with many toys that are still familiar today. They had hoops, stilts, marbles, dice, kites, pull toys, and yo-yos. Girls had dolls and boys had toy soldiers. Children loved to play ball games. Roman balls were made from different materials including wood, string, and leather stuffed with horsehair. Bouncy balls were made from a blown-up pig's bladder wrapped tightly in leather. Other games included hide-and-seek, blindman's bluff, and leap frog. P*ar impar* was a popular game where one child hid a number of stones or nuts in a fist, while another child had to guess whether the number was odd or even.

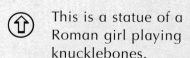
This is a statue of a Roman girl playing knucklebones.

Timeline

Glossary

amphitheater an oval-shaped, open-air stadium with an arena in the center surrounded by seats

architect a person who designs buildings

arena the central oval area of an amphitheater where shows and fights were staged

awning a covering made of material that is stretched across a frame

banned something is banned when it is prevented from happening or being used

cereals food made from grain, such as wheat, barley, or oats

chariot a small carriage usually with two wheels that is pulled by animals, often horses for racing

charioteers people who drive chariots

citizens a Roman citizen was originally a resident of Rome itself. Later, people all over the Roman Empire enjoyed the rights and privileges of being a Roman citizen.

comedies a comedy is a type of light-hearted performance that is designed to amuse people and make them laugh

gallies ancient ships with oars along each side, rowed by teams of oarsmen. Many galleys also had sails.

gladiators trained fighters who performed in an amphitheater. Gladiators were often slaves, convicts, or prisoners of war.

gridiron a metal grill

Latin the language spoken by the people who settled in Latium, a region in the west of central Italy

lyre a stringed instrument with a U-shaped frame, which is played by plucking

mime in Rome times, a type of comedy in which the actors spoke

plucking pulling sharply

republic a kind of government in which the citizens elect officials to represent them

rivalry competition between two opposing sides or people

senator a member of the Senate, the advisers to Roman rulers

social classes different ranks in society. A Roman's social class depended largely on their family and their wealth.

sponsor someone who pays for a project or activity

Syrian from Syria, a country in today's Middle East

tragedies a tragedy is a type of serious performance that often ends with the death of the main character

vibrate to move rapidly from side to side

Index

Resources and Web Sites

People of the Ancient World: The Ancient Romans by Allison Lassieur (Children's Press, 2005)

You Wouldn't Want to be a Roman Gladiator! by John Malam (Scholastic Library, 2001)

Web Sites

Due to the changing nature of Internet links, PowerKids Press has developed an online list of Web sites related to the subject of this book. This site is updated regularly. Please use this link to access this list: http://www.powerkidslinks.com/acrl/sports/